Dream Journal

Date ___/___/_____

Dream Title:
Setting(s):

Important dream imagery (Draw):

Characters:

Props or Symbols:

Emotions:

Personal Meaning / Notes:

Date ___/___/_____

Dream Title:

Setting(s):

Important dream imagery (Draw):

Characters:

Props or Symbols:

Emotions:

Personal Meaning / Notes:

Date ___/___/_____

Dream Title:

Setting(s):

Important dream imagery (Draw):

Characters:

Props or Symbols:

Emotions:

Personal Meaning / Notes:

Date ___/___/_____

Dream Title:

Setting(s):

Important dream imagery (Draw):

Characters:

Props or Symbols:

Emotions:

Personal Meaning / Notes:

Date ___/___/_____

Dream Title:

Setting(s):

Important dream imagery (Draw):

Characters:

Props or Symbols:

Emotions:

Personal Meaning / Notes:

Date ___/___/_____

Dream Title:
Setting(s):
Important dream imagery (Draw) :
Characters:
Props or Symbols:
Emotions:

Personal Meaning / Notes:

Date ___/___/_____

Dream Title:

Setting(s):

Important dream imagery (Draw) :

Characters:

Props or Symbols:

Emotions:

Personal Meaning / Notes:

Date ___/___/_____

Dream Title:
Setting(s):

Important dream imagery (Draw):

Characters:

Props or Symbols:

Emotions:

Personal Meaning / Notes:

Date ___/___/_____

Dream Title:

Setting(s):

Important dream imagery (Draw):

Characters:

Props or Symbols:

Emotions:

Personal Meaning / Notes:

Date ___/___/_____

Dream Title:

Setting(s):

Important dream imagery (Draw):

Characters:

Props or Symbols:

Emotions:

Personal Meaning / Notes:

Date ___/___/_____

Dream Title:

Setting(s):

Important dream imagery (Draw):

Characters:

Props or Symbols:

Emotions:

Personal Meaning / Notes:

Date ___/___/_____

Dream Title:
Setting(s):

Important dream imagery (Draw) :

Characters:

Props or Symbols:

Emotions:

Personal Meaning / Notes:

Date ___/___/_____

Dream Title:

Setting(s):

Important dream imagery (Draw):

Characters:

Props or Symbols:

Emotions:

Personal Meaning / Notes:

Date ___/___/_____

Dream Title:
Setting(s):

Important dream imagery (Draw):

Characters:

Props or Symbols:

Emotions:

Personal Meaning / Notes:

Date ___/___/_____

Dream Title:
Setting(s):

Important dream imagery (Draw):

Characters:

Props or Symbols:

Emotions:

Personal Meaning / Notes:

Date ___/___/_____

Dream Title:

Setting(s):

Important dream imagery (Draw) :

Characters:

Props or Symbols:

Emotions:

Personal Meaning / Notes:

Date ___/___/_____

Dream Title:

Setting(s):

Important dream imagery (Draw) :

Characters:

Props or Symbols:

Emotions:

Personal Meaning / Notes:

Date ___/___/_____

Dream Title:
Setting(s):

Important dream imagery (Draw):

Characters:

Props or Symbols:

Emotions:

Personal Meaning / Notes:

Date ___/___/_____

Dream Title:

Setting(s):

Important dream imagery (Draw):

Characters:

Props or Symbols:

Emotions:

Personal Meaning / Notes:

Date ___/___/_____

Dream Title:
Setting(s):
Important dream imagery (Draw) :
Characters:
Props or Symbols:
Emotions:

Personal Meaning / Notes:

Date ___/___/_____

Dream Title:

Setting(s):

Important dream imagery (Draw) :

Characters:

Props or Symbols:

Emotions:

Personal Meaning / Notes:

Date ___/___/_____

Dream Title:

Setting(s):

Important dream imagery (Draw):

Characters:

Props or Symbols:

Emotions:

Personal Meaning / Notes:

Date ___/___/_____

Dream Title:

Setting(s):

Important dream imagery (Draw):

Characters:

Props or Symbols:

Emotions:

Personal Meaning / Notes:

Date ___/___/_____

Dream Title:

Setting(s):

Important dream imagery (Draw):

Characters:

Props or Symbols:

Emotions:

Personal Meaning / Notes:

Date ___/___/_____

Dream Title:
Setting(s):

Important dream imagery (Draw) :

Characters:

Props or Symbols:

Emotions:

Personal Meaning / Notes:

Date ___/___/_____

Dream Title:
Setting(s):

Important dream imagery (Draw) :

Characters:

Props or Symbols:

Emotions:

Personal Meaning / Notes:

Date ___/___/_____

Dream Title:

Setting(s):

Important dream imagery (Draw) :

Characters:

Props or Symbols:

Emotions:

Personal Meaning / Notes:

Date ___/___/_____

Dream Title:

Setting(s):

Important dream imagery (Draw):

Characters:

Props or Symbols:

Emotions:

Personal Meaning / Notes:

Date ___/___/_____

Dream Title:
Setting(s):

Important dream imagery (Draw):

Characters:

Props or Symbols:

Emotions:

Personal Meaning / Notes:

Date ___/___/_____

Dream Title:

Setting(s):

Important dream imagery (Draw):

Characters:

Props or Symbols:

Emotions:

Personal Meaning / Notes:

Date ___/___/_____

Dream Title:
Setting(s):

Important dream imagery (Draw) :

Characters:

Props or Symbols:

Emotions:

Personal Meaning / Notes:

Date ___/___/_____

Dream Title:

Setting(s):

Important dream imagery (Draw):

Characters:

Props or Symbols:

Emotions:

Personal Meaning / Notes:

Date ___/___/_____

Dream Title:

Setting(s):

Important dream imagery (Draw):

Characters:

Props or Symbols:

Emotions:

Personal Meaning / Notes:

Date ___/___/_____

Dream Title:
Setting(s):

Important dream imagery (Draw) :

Characters:

Props or Symbols:

Emotions:

Personal Meaning / Notes:

Date ___/___/_____

Dream Title:

Setting(s):

Important dream imagery (Draw):

Characters:

Props or Symbols:

Emotions:

Personal Meaning / Notes:

Date ___/___/_____

Dream Title:

Setting(s):

Important dream imagery (Draw) :

Characters:

Props or Symbols:

Emotions:

Personal Meaning / Notes:

Date ___/___/_____

Dream Title:

Setting(s):

Important dream imagery (Draw) :

Characters:

Props or Symbols:

Emotions:

Personal Meaning / Notes:

Date ___/___/_____

Dream Title:
Setting(s):
Important dream imagery (Draw) :
Characters:
Props or Symbols:
Emotions:

Personal Meaning / Notes:

Date ___/___/_____

Dream Title:
Setting(s):

Important dream imagery (Draw):

Characters:

Props or Symbols:

Emotions:

Personal Meaning / Notes:

Date ___/___/_____

Dream Title:
Setting(s):

Important dream imagery (Draw) :

Characters:

Props or Symbols:

Emotions:

Personal Meaning / Notes:

Date ___/___/_____

Dream Title:
Setting(s):
Important dream imagery (Draw) :
Characters:
Props or Symbols:
Emotions:

Personal Meaning / Notes:

Date ___/___/_____

Dream Title:
Setting(s):

Important dream imagery (Draw) :

Characters:

Props or Symbols:

Emotions:

Personal Meaning / Notes:

Date ___/___/_____

Dream Title:
Setting(s):

Important dream imagery (Draw):

Characters:

Props or Symbols:

Emotions:

Personal Meaning / Notes:

Date ___/___/_____

Dream Title:
Setting(s):

Important dream imagery (Draw):

Characters:

Props or Symbols:

Emotions:

Personal Meaning / Notes:

Date ___/___/_____

Dream Title:
Setting(s):

Important dream imagery (Draw):

Characters:

Props or Symbols:

Emotions:

Personal Meaning / Notes:

Date ___/___/_____

Dream Title:
Setting(s):

Important dream imagery (Draw):

Characters:

Props or Symbols:

Emotions:

Personal Meaning / Notes:

Date ___/___/_____

Dream Title:
Setting(s):

Important dream imagery (Draw):

Characters:

Props or Symbols:

Emotions:

Personal Meaning / Notes:

Date ___/___/_____

Dream Title:

Setting(s):

Important dream imagery (Draw):

Characters:

Props or Symbols:

Emotions:

Personal Meaning / Notes:

Date ___/___/_____

Dream Title:

Setting(s):

Important dream imagery (Draw):

Characters:

Props or Symbols:

Emotions:

Personal Meaning / Notes:

Date ___/___/_____

Dream Title:

Setting(s):

Important dream imagery (Draw):

Characters:

Props or Symbols:

Emotions:

Personal Meaning / Notes:

Date ___/___/_____

Dream Title:

Setting(s):

Important dream imagery (Draw) :

Characters:

Props or Symbols:

Emotions:

Personal Meaning / Notes:

Date ___/___/_____

Dream Title:
Setting(s):

Important dream imagery (Draw) :

Characters:

Props or Symbols:

Emotions:

Personal Meaning / Notes:

Date ___/___/_____

Dream Title:
Setting(s):

Important dream imagery (Draw) :

Characters:

Props or Symbols:

Emotions:

Personal Meaning / Notes:

Date ___/___/_____

Dream Title:
Setting(s):
Important dream imagery (Draw) :
Characters:
Props or Symbols:
Emotions:

Personal Meaning / Notes:

Date ___/___/_____

Dream Title:
Setting(s):

Important dream imagery (Draw) :

Characters:

Props or Symbols:

Emotions:

Personal Meaning / Notes:

Date ___/___/_____

Dream Title:

Setting(s):

Important dream imagery (Draw):

Characters:

Props or Symbols:

Emotions:

Personal Meaning / Notes:

Date ___/___/_____

Dream Title:
Setting(s):

Important dream imagery (Draw):

Characters:

Props or Symbols:

Emotions:

Personal Meaning / Notes:

Date ___/___/_____

Dream Title:

Setting(s):

Important dream imagery (Draw):

Characters:

Props or Symbols:

Emotions:

Personal Meaning / Notes:

Date ___/___/_____

Dream Title:

Setting(s):

Important dream imagery (Draw) :

Characters:

Props or Symbols:

Emotions:

Personal Meaning / Notes:

Date ___/___/_____

Dream Title:
Setting(s):

Important dream imagery (Draw) :

Characters:

Props or Symbols:

Emotions:

Personal Meaning / Notes:

Date ___/___/_____

Dream Title:
Setting(s):

Important dream imagery (Draw) :

Characters:

Props or Symbols:

Emotions:

Personal Meaning / Notes:

Date ___/___/_____

Dream Title:
Setting(s):
Important dream imagery (Draw) :
Characters:
Props or Symbols:
Emotions:

Personal Meaning / Notes:

Date ___/___/_____

Dream Title:
Setting(s):

Important dream imagery (Draw):

Characters:

Props or Symbols:

Emotions:

Personal Meaning / Notes:

Date ___/___/_____

Dream Title:
Setting(s):
Important dream imagery (Draw) :
Characters:
Props or Symbols:
Emotions:

Personal Meaning / Notes:

Date ___/___/_____

Dream Title:
Setting(s):

Important dream imagery (Draw) :

Characters:

Props or Symbols:

Emotions:

Personal Meaning / Notes:

Date ___/___/_____

Dream Title:
Setting(s):

Important dream imagery (Draw):

Characters:

Props or Symbols:

Emotions:

Personal Meaning / Notes:

Date ___/___/_____

Dream Title:
Setting(s):

Important dream imagery (Draw):

Characters:

Props or Symbols:

Emotions:

Personal Meaning / Notes:

Date ___/___/_____

Dream Title:
Setting(s):

Important dream imagery (Draw):

Characters:

Props or Symbols:

Emotions:

Personal Meaning / Notes:

Date ___/___/_____

Dream Title:
Setting(s):
Important dream imagery (Draw) :
Characters:
Props or Symbols:
Emotions:

Personal Meaning / Notes:

Date ___/___/_____

Dream Title:
Setting(s):

Important dream imagery (Draw) :

Characters:

Props or Symbols:

Emotions:

Personal Meaning / Notes:

Date ___/___/_____

Dream Title:
Setting(s):
Important dream imagery (Draw) :
Characters:
Props or Symbols:
Emotions:

Personal Meaning / Notes:

Date ___/___/_____

Dream Title:
Setting(s):
Important dream imagery (Draw) :
Characters:
Props or Symbols:
Emotions:

Personal Meaning / Notes:

Date ___/___/_____

Dream Title:
Setting(s):

Important dream imagery (Draw) :

Characters:

Props or Symbols:

Emotions:

Personal Meaning / Notes:

The End

Made in the USA
Lexington, KY
19 December 2018